In Search of the

# DEADLY

## Factbook:
# >>>>> Bizarre Beasts

Look out for the other
DEADLY books:

# OUT NOW :

Deadly Factbook: Mammals
Deadly Factbook Minibeasts:
Spiders and Insects
Deadly Factbook:
Reptiles and Amphibians
Deadly Factbook: Fish,
Squid and Jellyfish

Deadly Activity Book
Deadly Brain Teasers
Deadly Colouring Book
Deadly Top 10
Deadly Doodle Books 1, 2, 3

Deadly Diaries
Deadly Detectives

BBC
EARTH

# DEADLY

## Factbook: >>>>> Bizarre Beasts

Orion
Children's Books

First published in Great Britain in 2014
by Orion Children's Books
a division of the Orion Publishing Group Ltd
Orion House
5 Upper St Martin's Lane
London WC2H 9EA
An Hachette UK Company

1 3 5 7 9 10 8 6 4 2

Photo credits

(b: bottom; t: top; l: left; r: right; c: centre)
**Ardea.com:** 16 D Parer & E. Parer-Cook; 18 Ken Lucas; 19 John Mason; 34 Nick Gordon; 58-59 Doc White; 72 Pat Morris; 78 Steve Downer. **BBC:** 2 © BBC 2009. **Corbis:** 17 Alex Wild/ Visuals Unlimited. **Naturepl.Com/BBC:** 1tr (&76-7) Patricio Robles Gil; 2 Steven David Miller; 25 Brendan Cole; 38 Steven David Miller; 40-41 Brandon Cole; 43 Solvin Zankl; 45 Martin Dohrn; 46-47 Nature Production; 50-51 Markus Varesvuo; 54-55 Wild Wonders of Europe/Zankl; 56 Solvin Zankl; 63 Alex Hyde; 67 John Downer; 68-69 Edwin Giesbers; 70-71 Mark Carwardine. **Photoshot/ NHPA:** 13 Nick Garbutt; 35 Daniel Heuclin. **Shutterstock.com:** 8-9 Nicolas.Voisin44; 22 Dmytro Pylypenko; 30 Ryan M. Bolton; 32 You Touch Pix of EuToch; 36 C.K.Ma. **Thinkstock:** Istock: 1b; 3; 6; 11; 20; 26; 27; 28-29; 37; 44; 48; 52-53; 60; 61; 64; 65; 66; 73; 74-75. Fuse14.

Compiled by Jinny Johnson     Designed by Sue Michniewicz

A catalogue record for this book is available from the British Library.

ISBN 978 1 4440 1004 6
Printed and bound in China

 **CONTENTS**

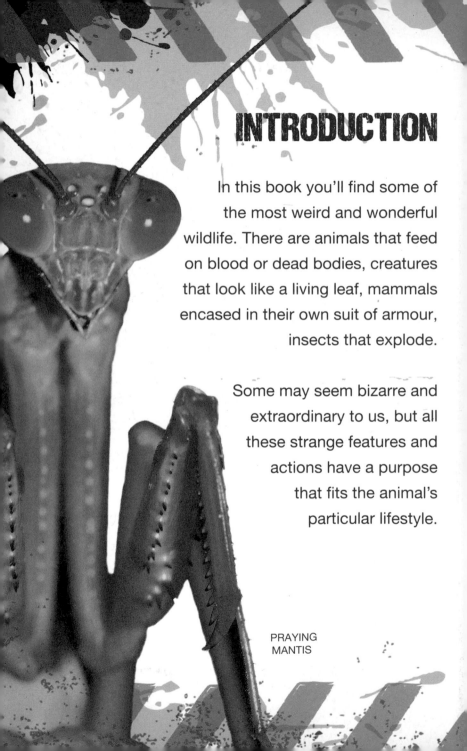

# INTRODUCTION

In this book you'll find some of the most weird and wonderful wildlife. There are animals that feed on blood or dead bodies, creatures that look like a living leaf, mammals encased in their own suit of armour, insects that explode.

Some may seem bizarre and extraordinary to us, but all these strange features and actions have a purpose that fits the animal's particular lifestyle.

PRAYING MANTIS

# WACKY WEAPONS

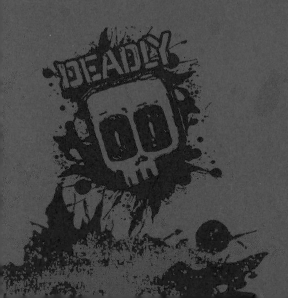

## Chapter 1

The **THRESHER SHARK**'s extraordinarily long tail fin is a lethal weapon. The shark uses its tail like a giant whip to herd small fish, such as sardines, together. It stuns and kills the fish with vicious blows of its tail, then catches them with its sharp teeth.

This huge shark can be up to 6 metres long,
its deadly tail fin making up half of this
length. It's known as the thresher shark
because its tail has a similar shape to
an old-fashioned scythe, used for
threshing or gathering crops.

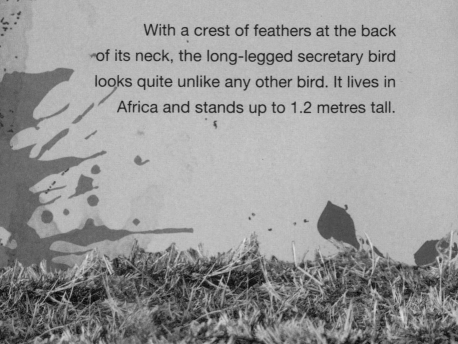

The **SECRETARY BIRD**'s weapons are its feet. The bird has a special way of killing prey. While many birds of prey soar high above the ground searching for food, the secretary bird prefers to walk. It marches around and when it comes across a mouse, frog, bird or even a snake, it stamps on it! Having crushed and killed the animal, the bird swallows it whole. It may also attack prey with its sharp beak.

With a crest of feathers at the back of its neck, the long-legged secretary bird looks quite unlike any other bird. It lives in Africa and stands up to 1.2 metres tall.

The **GHARIAL** is a master fisherman. It has a very long narrow snout which is lined with more than 100 super-sharp, interlocking teeth – ideal for seizing fish from the water with a speedy snap of those jaws. This expert predator is also one of the longest of all crocs and one of the fastest in water.

The male gharial has a lump on the end of its snout and the Indian name for this is ghara, meaning pot. This 'pot' may help the male attract females and he may even use it to make a humming sound while courting.

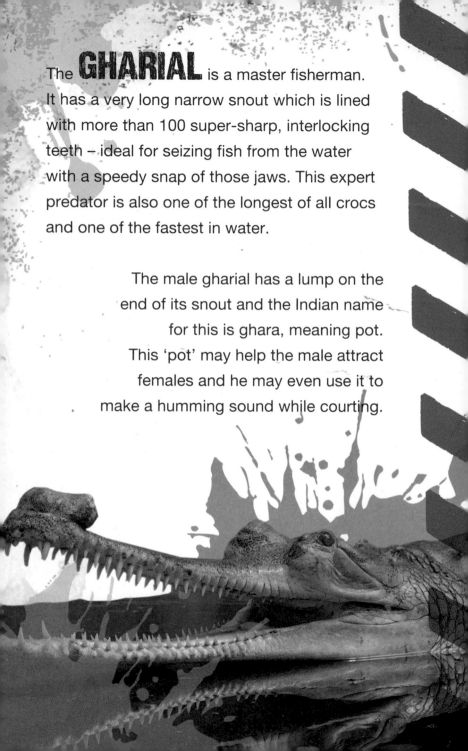

The **AYE-AYE** has an unusual deadly weapon – an extra-long finger that it uses to winkle insect larvae (young) out of wood. This curious creature lives in forests in Madagascar. It sleeps during the day, then wakes up at night to go hunting. First of all, the aye-aye taps on a tree trunk and listens for insect larvae scurrying beneath the bark. If it hears something, it tears away the bark with its teeth, then inserts its deadly finger to extract the prey.

You might be surprised to learn that the awesome aye-aye is a primate – a relative of monkeys and apes.

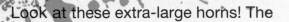
Look at these extra-large horns! The

# CAPE BUFFALO

is a plant-eater not a predator, but it is still one of the most formidable and dangerous animals in Africa. It can be very aggressive if threatened or startled and has been known to kill humans. Both male and female buffalo have horns but those of the male are larger. They measure as much as 1.4 metres across.

A buffalo can weigh as much as 12 people or more, and its massive bulk and massive horns make it a truly scary prospect. Buffalo travel in herds and together they can see off the fiercest predators – even big cats.

# FREAKY FOODS

DEADLY

Chapter 2

You've probably heard about the vampire bat, which feeds only on blood, but did you know that there is a blood-eating bird? The

# VAMPIRE FINCH,

also called the sharp-beaked ground finch, lives on the Galápagos Islands off the coast of South America. It usually feeds on seeds but sometimes during the dry season when seeds are scarce, it has a change of diet.

The finch pecks away at the back of a large seabird, such as a booby, until the blood starts to flow and then laps up the blood. The seabirds don't seem to mind much, unless the finch pecks too hard.

# The **DRACULA ANT**

is stranger still. These ants live in colonies of thousands of individuals. Like other ants, the workers go out hunting and bring food back to the nest for their young.

The odd thing is that the adult ants cannot eat solid food because their waist – the bit between the head and the body – is too narrow. They can only drink fluids. So to feed themselves, the worker ants chew holes in their well-fed larvae and suck out some of their body fluids, similar to blood. The larvae might not enjoy this but it doesn't kill them.

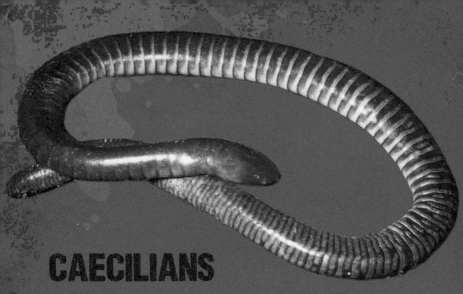

# CAECILIANS

might look like worms or snakes but in fact they are a kind of amphibian, like frogs. They are burrowers and live in tunnels underground, which they dig with the help of their strong pointy snout.

Adult caecilians hunt and eat insects, snakes, frogs and lizards, but the young of some kinds have a very unusual diet. The newly hatched caecilians, which look like tiny versions of their parents, eat the outer layer of their mother's skin, which contains lots of fat and goodness. The young even have special teeth for eating the skin. The mother regrows her outer skin every few days as her babies eat it up.

# BURYING BEETLES

feed on dead bodies, usually those of rodents or small birds that have died naturally.

When a pair of beetles finds a body, they bury it in the soil. They may need to move it to a suitable spot and they can carry a body that's up to 200 times their own weight.

Once the body is buried, the female beetle lays her eggs nearby. The rotting flesh provides plenty of food for her young once they hatch.

**VULTURES** are birds of prey but they find their food by scavenging. A scavenger is a creature that eats animals that are already dead, instead of hunting and killing.

Vultures have incredible eyesight and find their food by soaring high above the ground. Once a vulture spots something it makes a high-speed dive to the ground. This acts as a signal for other vultures and there will soon be a big gang of birds around the carcass.

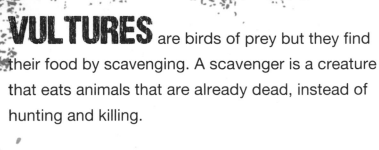

VULTURES

20

The vultures tear in with their brutal, bone-shredding beaks, pulling every scrap of meat from the bones. They will even climb inside the body. However rotten the flesh, the vultures still gobble it up.

One of the most bizarre of all creatures is a little worm called the

# BONE-EATING SNOT-FLOWER WORM.

These worms live in the ocean and feed on nutrients that are on and within the bones of whales that have died. The top of the worm looks like a flower covered in snot. The 'snot' is a ball of mucus that is thought to help protect the worm from predators.

The snowy

# SHEATHBILL

is a scavenger too.
This bird lives in the Antarctic
area and eats almost
anything it can find –
including seal poo and
penguin poo!

# CURIOUS CAMOUFLAGE

Chapter 3

The ability of the

# GIANT CUTTLEFISH

to hide itself in its surroundings is astonishing.
It can change colour in an instant, turning
from reddish-brown to yellow, white, red and
other hues. It can also change the texture of
its skin, raising areas of it to blend in against
the background and look like rocks, sand or
seaweed.

This colourful beast is the largest of the
cuttlefish – relatives of octopus and squid.
It grows to a metre or so long and weighs
10 kilograms.

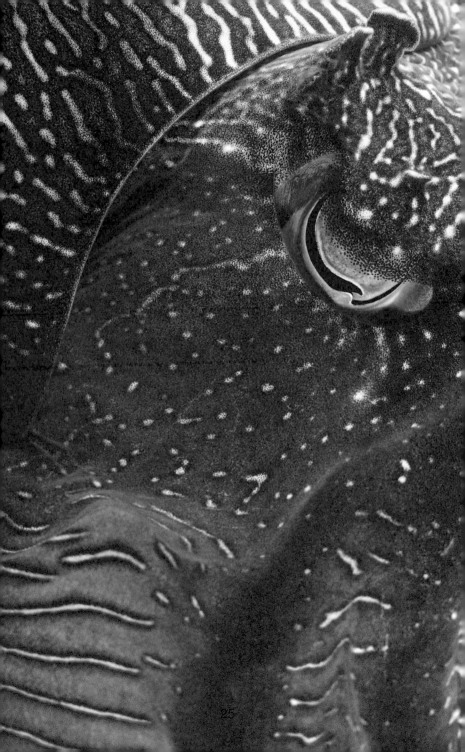

The **PRAYING MANTIS** is one of the fastest, most efficient of all insect hunters – and also one of the most weird in appearance. Its triangular head and huge eyes make it look like an alien but its long front legs, equipped with sharp spikes, are perfect weapons for grabbing prey at lightning speed.

The mantis relies on camouflage to keep itself hidden while lying in wait for prey. Many are green with a body shaped like a leaf, complete with vein-like markings. Others may be white or pink and are very hard to spot as they sit on orchid flowers.

The female mantis is particularly fierce. She generally eats the male after, or even during, mating!

# The LEAFY SEADRAGON

has some of the best
camouflage of any animal. This fish lives in
the sea among forests of kelp and other seaweed.
The many fronds hanging from its body make it look
almost exactly like the seaweed it lives among and
very hard for any hungry hunter to see.

The seadragon is a relative of the seahorse. The male
seadragon has a special spongy patch under his tail
with lots of tiny pits where the female puts her eggs
after mating. The male dragon carries the eggs here
while they develop.

Seadragons grow to about 30-43 centimetres long
and feed on minute sea creatures.

The **MATAMATA TURTLE** is another master of disguise. This creature lives in muddy rivers with lots of dead leaves and plants. Its knobbly, flattened body and leaf-shaped head adorned with flaps and fringes keep it well hidden as it lies in wait for prey such as fish or frogs.

This turtle also has its own built-in snorkel. It can lie in the water watching for prey with only its snout above the surface so it can breathe. When prey comes near, the turtle opens its very large mouth as wide as it can. Water and prey are sucked into the gaping jaws and the matamata quickly snaps them shut. The victim is swallowed whole and the water is pushed out from the side of its mouth.

The
# SATANIC LEAF-TAILED GECKO

is a camouflage champion.
Its twisted body looks incredibly
like a dead leaf and it is almost
impossible to see as it moves
around the rainforest
floor,
hunting
insects. Its tail
even has markings
like the veins of a leaf
and the edges look like
they have been nibbled by other creatures.

This gecko is up to 15 centimetres long
and lives only in Madagascar.

It has no proper eyelids so licks away
any dust or dirt in its eyes with its
super-long tongue.

DEADLY

# DEADLY DEFENDERS

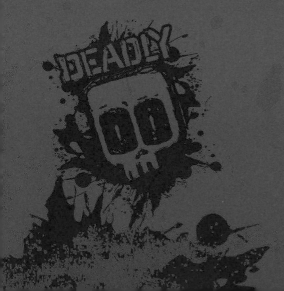

**Chapter 4**

# MALAYSIAN EXPLODING ANTS really do explode.

If a group of the ants meets rival ants, some of the workers create an explosion in their own bodies to save their companions.

This type of ant has extra-large glands in its body that make a poisonous, sticky substance. If in danger, some of the ants use special muscles to burst open their bodies, covering the enemy with the gungy poison. The exploded ants die but hopefully the rest are saved.

The **AFRICAN CRESTED PORCUPINE** is the largest porcupine in the world and, like all its family, it is a walking pincushion. Its name means 'thorny pig' but in fact the porcupine is a member of the rodent group, like rats and mice.

The porcupine's body is covered with sharp spines, called quills, which are up to 35 centimetres long – twice the size of a pencil. These can be raised and provide an effective defence against the fiercest of attackers.

If in danger, the first thing the porcupine does is to rattle its quills to warn off the attacker. If the enemy doesn't give up, the porcupine may charge backwards ramming its quills into the attacker. The quills drop out of the porcupine's skin easily, leaving the attacker with a sharp spike in its flesh which can cause a serious wound.

Even lions sometimes lose the battle against the prickly porcupine.

# The GOLIATH BIRD-EATING SPIDER

lives in the jungles of South America. If attacked, this deadly spider can bite, but it also has another way of warning enemies to leave it alone.

It is covered in tiny barbed hairs which it can kick off against an enemy. These can get into another animal's eyes, nose and mouth and cause intense irritation.
A spider to avoid!

DEADLY

**PITOHUIS** are among the very few known poisonous birds. They live in New Guinea and have poison in their feathers and skin. Scientists think that the toxins come from the beetles that the birds eat. The pitohui is unharmed by the toxins but they cause numbness and burning in the mouth of anything that tries to eat the bird.

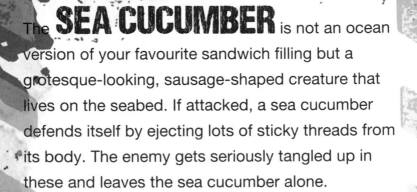

The **SEA CUCUMBER** is not an ocean version of your favourite sandwich filling but a grotesque-looking, sausage-shaped creature that lives on the seabed. If attacked, a sea cucumber defends itself by ejecting lots of sticky threads from its body. The enemy gets seriously tangled up in these and leaves the sea cucumber alone.

A relative of starfish and sea urchins, the sea cucumber gathers tiny animals and other food particles with small tentacle-like structures around its mouth. These are actually tube feet but are used for feeding.

There is a fish that finds the sea cucumber a life saver. The little pearl fish escapes predators by hiding away in a sea cucumber's bottom!

The **PANGOLIN** has its very own suit of armour. It is covered with overlapping scales, which make it look much like a walking pinecone. These tough scales are made of the same material as our hair and protect the animal from predators, as well as from the stings of its favourite food – ants and termites.

This insect-hunting mammal has strong claws for digging into insect nests and a tongue that can extend up to 25 centimetres to slurp up prey.

The **CASSOWARY** is a bizarre-looking bird and also very dangerous. Second only to the ostrich in weight, it is the heaviest bird in Australia and can weigh up to 76 kilograms – nearly as much as an average human.

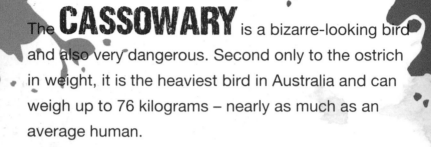

The bird cannot fly but can deliver a lethal kick. The inner toe on each of the cassowary's feet is equipped with a large sharp claw that can be up to 13 centimetres long. The bird can lash out with these claws and has been known to kill or seriously injure people.

The crest on the cassowary's head is called a casque and is made of keratin, like our fingernails.

# REMARKABLE HUNTERS

DEADLY 00

Chapter 5

# HUMPBACK WHALES rely

on some astonishing teamwork for successful
hunting, using an unusual technique called
bubble-net feeding.

Having found an area of water with lots of
shoaling fish such as herring, the whales dive
down and herd the fish together into a tightly
packed group. Another whale swims below the
fish and makes an incredibly loud call. The fish
panic and to escape this deafening sound they
start to swim towards the water surface.

Meanwhile, another humpback blows out a stream
of air to create a net of bubbles in the water.

As the fish swim up, they are trapped in the net of bubbles made by the whales and are promptly swallowed by the humpbacks as they come to the surface.

The humpback whale feeds by filtering fish and other small creatures from the water. Hanging from its upper jaw are large plates made of a hair-like substance. There are as many as 400 of these baleen plates and they are up to 76 centimetres long.  The whale takes in a huge mouthful of water and food. As the water flows through the baleen, any food items are trapped and then swallowed.

The humpback whale is up to 17 metres long. Its flippers can be 5 metres long and are the longest flippers of any animal.

The **GANNET** is a beautiful seabird that dives like a missile when hunting. The bird soars high above the ocean searching for prey. When it spots something it makes a super-speedy dive down to the sea and plunges into the water at 100 kilometres an hour to seize its catch.

To protect it as it dives, the gannet has an extra-hard skull and special air-filled sacs under the skin of the face and chest to cushion the impact.

A large aggressive seabird, the **SKUA** is a flying pirate. It watches out for other seabirds carrying food back to their nests and then attacks in midair. The fierce skua harasses the other bird, forcing it to give up its catch. The skua will even make another bird regurgitate its meal and then eats that up.

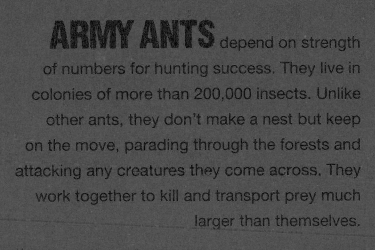

**ARMY ANTS** depend on strength of numbers for hunting success. They live in colonies of more than 200,000 insects. Unlike other ants, they don't make a nest but keep on the move, parading through the forests and attacking any creatures they come across. They work together to kill and transport prey much larger than themselves.

In one day a colony of army ants may catch as many as 30,000 prey.

The
# JAPANESE GIANT HORNET
is one of the fiercest and deadliest of all insects.
Its body can be up to 5 centimetres long, wingspan
reaches 7.5 centimetres and it has a sting that injects
powerful venom.

The hornets attack bees' nests and can kill thousands of bee larvae in a matter of minutes.

DEADLY

But scientists have made a fantastic discovery. The bees fight back. A mob of bees can surround a hornet in a tightly packed ball, killing the deadly attacker.

The huge beak of the

# GROUND HORNBILL

might look awkward but in fact it is a superb
precision tool for attacking prey on the ground.

The hornbill can fly but it prefers to hunt on foot
and snakes are one of its favourite foods. When it
finds a snake, the hornbill makes a speedy strike
straight for the head and attacks with its strong
sharp beak. This is a wise move, particularly
with a venomous snake. If the bird attacked the
snake's tail, the reptile could wriggle round and
deliver a deadly bite.

Both male and female
have bare skin on the face.
The female's skin is violet
in colour but the male's is
bright red. Check out
the hornbill's eyelashes
too. They are very
long and perfect for
protecting the eyes
from dust.

# STRANGE SENSES

DEADLY
00

**Chapter 6**

The **GREAT GREY OWL**'s round, flattened face is this shape for a reason. The face acts like a satellite dish to give the bird something like surround-sound hearing.

The ring of feathers
collects the tiniest noise and
channels it to the ears hidden on each side of the
face. This enables the owl to pick up the slightest
squeak or scuffle made by a mouse on the ground.

Having pinpointed its prey, the owl swoops down
to seize its meal. Its soft-edged feathers allow it fly
silently and take its prey by surprise.

The **FENNEC FOX** 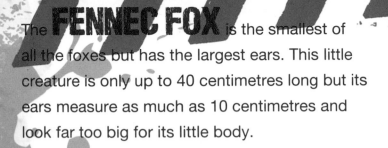 is the smallest of all the foxes but has the largest ears. This little creature is only up to 40 centimetres long but its ears measure as much as 10 centimetres and look far too big for its little body.

This fox lives in the deserts of North Africa and really needs its big ears. First of all they help it hear the slightest sound of prey moving in the sand. Also they act like cooling devices to help the fox lose heat in the scorching daytime temperatures.

**SWORDFISH** are large fast-moving predators that patrol the world's oceans for prey. Scientists believe that these fish are able to heat up their eyes to improve their vision in cold water, and so help them track speedy prey.

A swordfish can grow up to 4.5 metres long. It has a long sword-like beak which it uses to spear prey or slashes through the water to kill other fish.

The eyes of the **OCTOPUS** may look extraordinary but they are amazingly similar to our own.

Like us, the octopus has 2 eyes and each has an iris, pupil and lens. It is believed to have good sight.

Octopus and squid have larger brains than any other invertebrate animal.

DEADLY

The **MANTIS SHRIMP** is less than 30 centimetres long but its eyes are among the most complex of any animal. The eyes stand on stalks and can move independently of each other, making the shrimp look like a mini robot.

The mantis shrimp can also see things with 3 different parts of each eye and its colour vision is far more sophisticated than ours.

Would you believe that this shrimp also packs a powerful punch? It hits out at prey with a blow powerful enough to smash the shells of crabs and snails. Its blow is one of the fastest in the animal kingdom. When it strikes, it moves its arm at as much as 80 kilometres an hour.

# BIZARRE BODIES

## Chapter 7

Unicorns are mythical creatures, but there is a kind of whale called the

# NARWHAL

that is sometimes known as the 'unicorn of the sea'.

This is because
the male has a single
long spiral tusk – like a unicorn.

The tusk is actually one of the whale's
2 teeth and can grow to as much as
2.5 metres long. Some females have a
tusk but this is usually shorter than a male's.

No one knows quite why the narwhal
has this long tusk. People used to think it
might be a weapon or a tool for spearing food,
but it is more likely a way of attracting
mates. Females may choose the males
with the longest tusks.

The **PUFFIN** has one of the wackiest beaks in the bird world. But the beak is not quite as bright all year round. It fades in the winter and becomes more colourful in the spring, before the breeding season, so experts think the colours may help a puffin attract mates.

At other times this large beak is very useful for carrying fish. A puffin can hold lots of fish at once in its beak and carry them back to its young. The puffin's rough tongue helps hold the fish in place against spines in the beak while it snaps up more.

Who do you think
has the most legs of any animal? It's a

# MILLIPEDE,

which is a long, worm-like animal. But while
most millipedes have about 100 legs, there is
one that is only 3 centimetres long but has as
many as 750 legs. Scientists thought that this
millipede, called *Illacme plenipes*, was extinct,
but it has recently been found in California.

The millipede also spins silk
which it uses to make a kind of cloak
over its body.

The **FOSSA** might look like a cat with a long tail like a monkey, but actually this fierce hunter is a relative of the meerkat and belongs to Madagascar's mongoose family.

The fossa lives only in Madagascar where it is the largest carnivore. It hunts on the ground and in trees, catching anything from mice to lemurs. Its long tail helps it balance as it runs along branches and jumps from tree to tree.

# The DUCK-BILLED PLATYPUS

is such an outlandish beast that when specimens were first brought to Britain from Australia scientists thought it was a trick. They thought someone had put together bits and pieces from several animals and added a duck's beak. In fact, the platypus's beak is a highly sensitive tool with electroreceptors that the animal uses to find prey in muddy water. The male platypus also has a spur on each hind leg that can inject poison into an attacker.

One of the other unusual things about the platypus is that it is one of only 2 types of mammal that lay eggs instead of bearing live young. The other is the echidna, or spiny anteater, which also lives in Australia.

One of the most peculiar
of all monkeys, the male

# PROBOSCIS
# MONKEY

has a very large nose. No one
knows quite why, but it may
help the male attract mates.
Female proboscis monkeys
seem to prefer males
with big noses.

This monkey also has a
very big tummy. This is not
because it is greedy but
because the leaves it
eats release lots of
gas as they are
digested, blowing
up the belly. This
must feel very
uncomfortable!

The **TURKEY VULTURE** is a big bird with wings which measure as much as 1.7 metres when fully spread – that's almost as long as a bed. It feeds on carrion and, unlike most birds, uses its sense of smell to find food.

The bird also has a weird way of keeping cool – it wees on to its legs. As the wee dries and evaporates, it cools the vulture's body. Scientists think that this strange habit has another purpose. The wee contains very strong stomach acids, which may kill any nasty bacteria that the bird has on its legs after stepping on rotting carcasses.

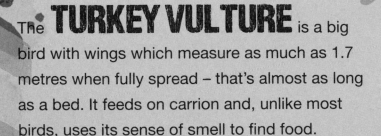

Did you know that there is a lizard with wings?

The **FLYING LIZARD** spends most of its life in rainforest trees, hunting insects.

To move from tree to tree or escape from predators, the lizard takes to the air instead of going all the way down to the ground. As it leaps off a branch it extends flaps of skin at the sides of its body. These 'wings' act like a kind of parachute and allow the lizard to glide gently through the air to another branch. It may travel as far as 9 metres.

A flying lizard grows to about 20 centimetres long including its tail.

The brilliantly coloured
# STRAWBERRY
# POISON-DART FROG
is small enough to sit on a penny
but has deadly poison in its skin.
The colour warns potential predators
that the frog will not taste good.
Also, the brighter the skin the better
– when females are choosing mates
they select the males with
the brightest colour.

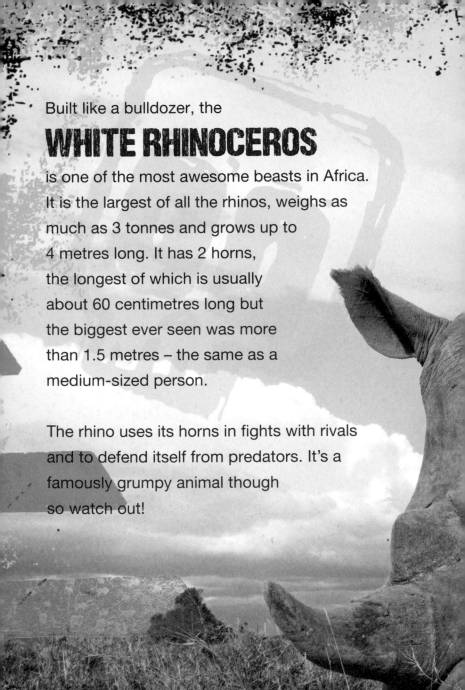

Built like a bulldozer, the

# WHITE RHINOCEROS

is one of the most awesome beasts in Africa.
It is the largest of all the rhinos, weighs as
much as 3 tonnes and grows up to
4 metres long. It has 2 horns,
the longest of which is usually
about 60 centimetres long but
the biggest ever seen was more
than 1.5 metres – the same as a
medium-sized person.

The rhino uses its horns in fights with rivals
and to defend itself from predators. It's a
famously grumpy animal though
so watch out!

One of the oddest looking of all birds, the **SHOEBILL** has an enormous beak that measures more than 20 centimetres long and over 10 centimetres wide. The beak is tipped with a sharp hook that the bird uses to attack prey such as fish, frogs and lizards.

The **KING VULTURE**'s head is brightly coloured but bald of feathers. The bird is a scavenger, which means it feeds on the bodies of dead animals, tearing them open with its strong hooked beak. The lack of feathers on the head may help the bird stay clean as it feeds. This vulture also has a keen sense of smell that helps it find its food.

The **MANDRILL** is one of the largest of all monkeys and also the most brightly coloured. A male has blue markings on his face, red nose and lips and a golden beard. When he's excited the colours become even brighter. The female has duller markings.

The mandrill has cheek pouches and can stuff these with food to enjoy later. Like other monkeys, mandrills eat lots of nuts and fruit, but they also hunt small animals.

An Australian lizard called the

# THORNY DEVIL

is a very remarkable reptile. Its body is
covered in sharp spines making it very
hard for any predator to attack.

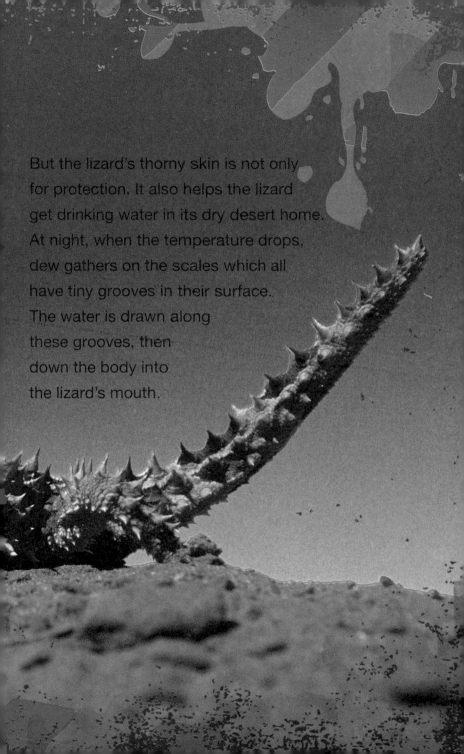

But the lizard's thorny skin is not only
for protection. It also helps the lizard
get drinking water in its dry desert home.
At night, when the temperature drops,
dew gathers on the scales which all
have tiny grooves in their surface.
The water is drawn along
these grooves, then
down the body into
the lizard's mouth.

The **VAMPIRE SQUID** is one of the strangest creatures in the sea. It eats stuff that other creatures don't want, such as poo and bits of dead fish and shellfish. It has 8 arms that are connected by webbing, as well as 2 extra- long structures that can be folded up in special pockets or stretched out to as much as 8 times the animal's length.

This fantastic creature lives in the deep, dark depths of the ocean and it has huge eyes – possibly the biggest for its size of any animal. It also has light organs all over its body and arms that glow in the dark water. If in danger, the vampire squid can turn itself inside out, inverting its webbed arms over itself like a cloak.

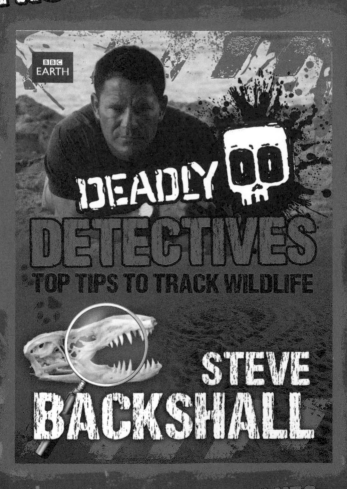

Become a detective with
# The DEADLY Team

BBC
EARTH

DEADLY

DETECTIVES

TOP TIPS TO TRACK WILDLIFE

STEVE
BACKSHALL

SPOT FASCINATING CLUES
IN THE NATURAL WORLD . . .